A GRINGO'S GUIDE TO ONLINE HISPANIC MARKETING

Brian Krogstad & Miles Houck

GENERATION EQUIS
MEDIA

A GRINGO'S GUIDE TO ONLINE HISPANIC MARKETING

PROVEN INTERNET BUSINESS & MARKETING STRATEGIES
TO CAPITALIZE ON THE EMERGING HISPANIC MARKET

Brian Krogstad & Miles Houck

Contributions by:
Mark Fischer
Anthony Coglianese
Anabel Birt Mosqueda
Jon Shulin
Shannon Maas

A GRINGO'S GUIDE TO ONLINE HISPANIC MARKETING

Copyright © 2010 by Generation Equis Media

Brian Krogstad & Miles Houck

Library of Congress Control Number: 2010902949

Printed in the United States of America

First Printing: March 2010

ISBN-13: 978-0-9844544-8-8

ISBN-10: 0-9844544-8-9

Ordering Information

Quantity sales and special discounts are available on quantity purchases by corporations, associations, and others.

For permission to reproduce the information in this publication for commercial redistribution, or for quantity sales and discounts, please contact us via email at:

Marketing@GenerationEquisMedia.com.

www.GenerationEquisMedia.com

ABOUT THE AUTHORS

Brian Krogstad

Brian Krogstad is a Sales and Marketing Specialist currently based in California. Since 1995 he has been a pioneer creating successful sales and marketing organizations for Fortune 500 and start-up companies. He is fluent in English as well as Spanish. Brian has done business in both Spain and Puerto Rico and has lived abroad and worked professionally in Mexico.

Miles Houck

Miles Houck is a Business and Technology professional who graduated college in Pennsylvania and now resides in California. Miles has helped Fortune 500 and start-up companies implement leading edge technologies and business concepts since 1984. Miles' passion is helping domestic and international businesses benefit from emerging market opportunities.

Brian and Miles, who are both members of Generation X, co-authored this book to share their in-depth knowledge of the emerging Hispanic market with business leaders and others who are interested in capitalizing on this growing market opportunity. Will you or your business be ready?

PREFACE

We have watched markets emerge and helped numerous companies succeed over the past twenty-five years. We decided to write this book to help the reader understand both the growing Hispanic market opportunity, and the effective business and marketing strategies we developed that target this ethnic group. The group is referred to as Generation Equis (pronounced: EH-kees) or Gen-Equis. The name represents those born after 1960 who are of Hispanic or Spanish origin. We use the Spanish pronunciation of the letter X – 'Equis'. This is similar to the well-known Generation X population born after 1960 but Gen-Equis is focused on the growing Hispanic population.

We draw on a vast amount of knowledge gained over the years when marketing to, and doing business with, different cultures. This book is an introduction and a guide to how the reader and any business organization they touch can do better when selling, servicing or marketing to the Generation Equis population group. The focus of the book is how to effectively use the Internet to reach this group. We provide complete information on strategies that any business or individual that desires to use the Internet to reach Generation Equis must understand.

This book was written using real world knowledge that was sometimes painful to obtain and required countless hours and dollars to perfect. Through our personal and professional adventures we learned many lessons and will share those that apply to Generation Equis.

We would like to thank the many people we have done business with and encountered over the years. We shared life experiences with many who helped us learn and gain understanding of other cultures. They enabled the foundation for this book.

There are far too many names to mention. Just the memories alone make us smile. If you remember either of us, we hope you are also smiling as you read this.

TABLE OF CONTENTS

INTRODUCTION

MEET GENERATION EQUIS

"Generation Equis – The fastest growing secret in America"

Whether you are a gringo (not of Hispanic, Latino or Spanish origin) or of any heritage - it is really unimportant. Our intent is not to use this term in a negative manner. We wanted to capture the attention of those who are not of Hispanic or Spanish origin as they stand to benefit the most by fully understanding Generation Equis and the potential of this untapped market. Our non-gringo, Generation Equis friends, will certainly also benefit from this book by marketing to Generation Equis.

You may not be aware that Generation Equis is perhaps one of the most rapidly growing population groups seen in the last century. They represent an incredible opportunity for any business or individual who learns how to effectively market, service and sell to them. This is the first of many books that will give you the insight that you need. The focus of this book is on how you can best use the Internet to target this group while also

1

providing insight into other traditional business and marketing approaches.

Who Is Generation Equis?

Generation Equis is a label given to the generation of individuals of Hispanic or Spanish origin who were born after 1960. Though members of this generation reside in many countries throughout the world, our particular focus for this book is the growing Hispanic segment of Generation X, referred to as Generation Equis, who lives and works in the United States.

To help you fully appreciate this future opportunity, we'll first take a brief look at history. We will dispel some common myths surrounding Generation X in the United States.. Then we will go into greater detail about their Hispanic equivalent - Generation Equis.

Generation X Definition

During the twentieth century, American historians and social commentators placed labels on various generations to quantify or label them for reference purposes. Today, Generation X is most commonly used to describe the nearly 80 million people born during the 1960s and 1970s.

Generation X was once thought to be lazy or unfocused. Though, as we look at their accomplishments, this proves to be a misleading negative concept introduced by the media early on. Over time, Generation X has now come to be viewed as:

- Ambitious

- Determined

- Creative

- Self Taught and Independent

- Diversified

Generation X, is one of the most entrepreneurial and technology friendly generations in American history. Why? Just look at how they have driven a majority of technological advancements enabling America to undergo rapid and significant advances. The most substantial include the personal computer and the Internet's astonishing growth and popularity. Many billion-dollar companies such as Microsoft, Dell, MySpace and YouTube, to name a few, were founded by people belonging to the Generation X demographic.

Generation Equis Definition

Generation Equis is, quite simply, the Hispanic equivalent of Generation X . This diverse group shares many traits with Generation X, but is unique in the following ways:

- Solid culture bonds them to their respective country of origin.

- Strong family values and unity are the norm.

- Being community minded – they choose to support their community.

- A determined work ethic is typical.

- Desire to do what it takes to earn and live the American Dream.

- Pride in ownership, education and entrepreneurialism.

- Their origin is from over twenty countries, unified by a common Spanish language foundation, including Central and South America, the Caribbean, and Spain.

- They speak Spanish, English, or both.

The growth potential of Generation Equis is equal or greater than that of their Generation X counterpart. We will expand on this in the sections that follow. In essence, they represent the same fundamentals and work values that enabled America to have unprecedented growth over the last one hundred years. Keep this in mind as you also realize their population group is consistently growing at a faster rate than Generation X or any other similar group in America.

The Demographic of Generation Equis

It is important to understand the people that make up Generation Equis, their culture, as well as the growth trend of this population both in number and in their use of the Internet. Generation Equis includes Spanish Speaking Immigrants, Temporary Hispanic Workers, and Chicanos (second & third generation born to Hispanic Immigrants).

As we pointed out in our definition of Generation Equis - their culture is very similar in many ways to the culture that formed the foundation for America. They are characterized by a hard-working spirit combined with strong family values and a solid sense of community – the very fundamentals that enabled America to grow substantially over the past one hundred years.

The population growth trend of Generation Equis in the United States is rapid and continuous. See **Table I.1**.

Table I.1: Generation Equis in America – Population Growth Trend

Census Year	US Total Population	US Hispanic Population	% Hispanic Growth	% of Total Population
1970	203,302,031	9,589,216		
1980	226,545,805	14,608,673	52.3	6.5
1990	248,709,873	22,354,059	53	9
2000	281,421,906	35,300,000	57.9	12.5

Source: U.S. Census Bureau (2000)

In an early 2010 speech, United States President Barack Obama estimated that there are eighteen million Hispanics who may have entered the country without following appropriate immigration guidelines; this statement implies that these "illegal immigrants" are not being counted in the Census. Thus in reality, the Hispanic population, or Generation Equis is even greater than the actual Census numbers indicate.

One in six people living in the United States is of Hispanic origin and this number could soon be one in five or less; according to the current growth trend, the Hispanic population nearly doubles every ten years. Though the 2010 Census data was not available at the time of publication of this book, we expect it to reveal a similar trend in the growth of this population.

So when you ask yourself "Who is Generation Equis?" just look around—they are the people all around you. They are a significant and rapidly growing population with the potential to play an expanding role in the United States and global marketplace.

This book focuses on how to benefit from this emerging market and enable Generation Equis to contribute and benefit as well.

The Buying Power of Generation Equis

T he Hispanic population in the United States alone represents incredible buying power - and that power is increasing daily - even during times of recession. Why? It is a combination of their population growth and determination to create a better life for themselves and their families. Sound like a familiar pattern? It should. These are the same qualities that fueled growth in the United States and allowed it to become the great nation it is today.

The combined buying power of Generation Equis will exceed one trillion dollars in 2010. This is nearly five times what it was in 1990, based on an estimate by the Selig Center for Economic Growth **(Table I.2)**. Quite simply, Generation Equis has buying power that exceeds all other minority groups.

Table I.2: Generation Equis in America – Hispanic Buying Power

Census Year	Hispanic Buying Power (billions of dollars)
1990	211.9
2000	489.5
2008	951.0
*2013	*1,386.2

Source: Selig Center for Economic Growth, Terry College of Business,
The University of Georgia (2008)
*2013 data is an estimated projection

We will not go into detail on the buying power of Generation Equis in this book. If you need convincing - feel free to use your

A GRINGO'S GUIDE TO ONLINE HISPANIC MARKETING

favorite web search engine and look for "Hispanic US buying power". You can find a wealth of supporting information to include their buying power and the significant growth expected over the next ten to twenty years.

Our focus for this book is on how to capitalize on this market. So let's continue with that in mind.

Who Is Benefiting Today

Many businesses today are benefiting from Generation Equis as a byproduct of their traditional business model. Frequently, these companies do not realize what a large piece of their market share, revenues and recruiting base this group truly represents.

The real question is which businesses decide to gain incremental revenue, dedicated employees and customer loyalty by targeting Generation Equis, and which companies will be impacted when their competition steps up to the plate and reaches out to this group first.

Some companies are finally taking notice. According to HispanicBusiness.com, advertisers are now spending billions to market to Hispanics. This trend has continued upward with increased spending of over five percent per year for the past five years.

However, some of the major Fortune 500 companies, as well as small to mid-sized companies, have been hesitant to invest a large amount of capital or resources in targeting this group, because they are making their business decisions based on the outdated 2000 Census data.

Instead of waiting for the 2010 Census data to show the unprecedented Hispanic population and buying power increases that have been projected, other forward-thinking companies and executives are using estimates, surveys and common sense to understand the potential of this untapped market and beat their competitors to market with a solid Generation Equis business strategy today.

Businesses that are ahead of the curve and are already actively targeting and enjoying the benefits of serving Generation Equis include: Geico Insurance (**Figure I.1**), Bank of America (**Figure I.2**), and IBM (**Figure I.3**).

The list of early adopters is growing rapidly. There will be many to follow and those that do not act will be less competitive and could lose substantial market share for their business.

Figure I.1: Generation Equis Friendly Companies – Geico

Source: www.migeico.com

Figure I.2: Generation Equis Friendly Companies – Bank of America

Source: www.bankofamerica.com

Figure I.3: Generation Equis Friendly Companies – IBM

Source: www.ibm.com

A GRINGO'S GUIDE TO ONLINE HISPANIC MARKETING

How You Too Can Benefit

The best way to benefit is to get started. Work on your plan and read on...Those who do not target this market are missing out. It is estimated, based on census data and independent research that over 10 percent of the buying power in the United States belongs to Hispanics - Generation Equis. As the population group grows at 50 percent annually, and their income levels increase, this percentage will continue to grow at an astounding rate.

It is just like investing: when the cashier at the local grocery store is telling you to buy a stock, it is time to sell. Timing is everything when considering tapping this ripe market. It is imperative that you be an industry leader and not a follower, to create and implement a successful Generation Equis business strategy that will make you stand out as a pioneer in your industry.

The time is now to target Generation Equis. Are you and your business ready to benefit?

CHAPTER ONE

ONLINE BUSINESS STRATEGIES

"Generation Equis – nontraditional business with a nontraditional market"

You may be looking to create an online presence or are ready to expand your existing online presence to reach out to Generation Equis. To succeed in either case you must understand the subtle and major differences between traditional online business and a Generation Equis-focused online business.

The sheer numbers and buyer power represented by Generation Equis are just too large to ignore. Internet powerhouses like Google, Yahoo and MSN have growing Spanish language search engines - primarily serving the United States. They also have indexed and return millions of results for Spanish and bilingual search strings while profiting from the sponsored Spanish Pay Per Click (PPC) ads that they present to web surfers.

We have found that Generation Equis has migrated to and embraced the Internet in the same fashion as other mainstream consumers. Yet mainstream companies have been slow in recognizing this opportunity and effectively marketing their products and services online with this powerful demographic in mind.

The first place to look when targeting Generation Equis, is your web presence. Translating your content to Spanish and putting a link to either a Spanish or English version of your website just is not enough. As you discovered in the first chapter of this book, Generation Equis represents more than just Spanish-speaking consumers. Generation Equis is a diverse demographic of English-speaking, Spanish-speaking and bilingual consumers that identifies themselves as Hispanic.

As we described earlier, Generation Equis is comprised of consumers from many different countries throughout Latin America and Europe and even from the United States as first and second generation Americans. This represents a challenge for most marketers who try to reach out to Generation Equis, because their target market is comprised of multiple cultures, dialects, and stages of assimilation.

We have found that focusing on the commonality of this demographic while respecting its diversity to be the best strategy in implementing a successful Generation Equis focused web strategy.

The key strategies to consider when doing business online with Generation Equis are:

• **Spanish Website Development:** From landing pages to a complete Spanish website integrated with an English website; the right website development strategy and relevant content are the initial consideration when doing business online with Generation Equis.

• **Metrics & Reporting:** If you have made the investment of time and money in building a new website, or modifying your existing website to target Generation Equis, you cannot make marketing decisions, establish metrics and benchmarks or even identify areas for improvement unless you have reliable information about visitor behavior.

• **Search Engine Optimization (SEO):** Optimizing your website, or individual web pages, for first page search engine ranking in both the English and Spanish search engines is key to introducing your brand, product or service to Generation Equis via the Internet. Search engines will provide you with the most cost effective and targeted traffic on the web.

• **Online Messaging:** Whenever you are messaging to the visitors to your website, whether you are using email communication or have implemented opt-in methods such as newsletters, it is important to track your visitors' preferences and "speak their language." For example, if a visitor signs up for a newsletter on your Spanish website they will expect it to be delivered to them in Spanish and the content be culturally relevant to Generation Equis, as defined by the nature of your business and the knowledge of the market that you take away from this book.

• **Internet Marketing:** Depending on budget, the right combination of Pay-Per-Click (PPC) and banner advertising, link exchanges, forum and blog posts and traditional media advertising can drive immediate traffic to your website and help you reach out to Generation Equis.

• **Social Networking:** It is hard to miss the social media craze that has swept through the mainstream Internet.

Generation Equis is taking advantage of both the Spanish version of English sites such as MySpace, Facebook and LinkedIn as well as the Spanish social media sites such as Sonico and Tuenti. In today's world, an online community or social networking presence is just as important to the success of your business as a physical community presence is.

In the following chapters, we will explore in greater detail how to execute on each of the strategies outlined above. You will get concrete tips and tactics you can employ to set your company up for success with Generation Equis.

A GRINGO'S GUIDE TO ONLINE HISPANIC MARKETING

CHAPTER TWO

SPANISH WEBSITE DEVELOPMENT

"Generation Equis – America's untapped Spanish speaking market"

The first step to doing business online with Generation Equis is developing a Spanish website or a Spanish landing page. Although a lot of members of Generation Equis speak and read English, they generally appreciate, and in some case prefer, a Spanish website. A Spanish website will also allow you to reach the truly untapped piece of Generation Equis; the Spanish-speaking Hispanics in America.

Whether the Spanish website complements an existing English website or will be your only online presence, it cannot simply be a translated clone of your English site. The most important thing to remember from the beginning of the project is to start from scratch!

Building a website that takes into account the unique culture you are targeting means more than just translating the text of your English site into Spanish. Generation Equis, like any customers, will do more business with you when they firmly understand your offerings and when you show that you firmly understand them.

The key strategies to consider when developing a Spanish website for Generation Equis are:

- **Start From Scratch:** A successful Spanish website needs to be a standalone site that may or may not be integrated into an existing English website with links. Simply translating the text of an English site into Spanish is not always the best option when reaching out to Generation Equis online.

- **The Planning Phase:** The most important phase of launching a Spanish website is the planning phase. You must define clear and achievable goals and, as early in the process as possible, work with a fully bilingual developer who understands the language and culture of Generation Equis as well as the ins and outs of dealing with your company's management.

- **Look & Feel:** The structure, style, color and images of your site need to appeal to the commonalties and cultural similarities of Generation Equis without isolating, insulting or offending members of the demographic.

- **Content is Key:** As with any website, content is a key factor in launching a successful Spanish website. Whether you organize focus groups, perform market research or just look at what content is used by the high page rank Spanish sites for ideas - the same goals should be kept in mind. First, make sure the content you select fits your business model and be careful to only use content that is attractive to Generation Equis and will prompt them to remember your brand, follow your call to action and return to your site.

• **Your Product and Services Offering:** Whether Generation Equis is a new untapped market for you, or it is an existing market where you would like to provide better service or increase your market penetration, it is imperative that you analyze your mainstream offerings for incremental opportunities specific to Generation Equis.

Now we will go into more detail about each of these topics.

Starting From Scratch

Many companies make the mistake of trying to translate their English website to Spanish without understanding the cultural differences and content requirements of a Spanish site or the pieces that are lost in translation. Companies that take this approach often end up scrapping the project and starting over when they do not get the results they want, losing the time and money invested in the initial project.

To design an effective Spanish-language website, you must have clear and concise goals, a culturally-aware content strategy and a launch point, or BETA release, before you start development. Investing time and resources at the planning stage will save you countless hours of rework, and keep you from potentially alienating the Hispanic market with a poorly planned, culturally insensitive site.

The Planning Phase

After setting the goals of your site, the next step is assembling the project team. Ideally, you should use a bilingual developer and a bilingual project or program manager. It is important to have someone driving the project who understands the languages and cultures represented by Generation Equis and can effectively communicate this information with the English speaking members of your company.

Have you ever called for technical support and talked with an outsourced technician with a thick accent and poor to fair English skills? It can be hard enough to understand the technical jargon without having to deal with a language barrier as well.

If you have an in-house IT or design department staffed with a superstar bilingual employee you may already have the right person for the job. Chances are, however, that your project will be more successful and cost effective if you outsource it to a bilingual web developer with a deep understanding of the market.

Research what your competitors are doing and see how many of them have Spanish websites. Be sure to note, bookmark, or add to favorites the sites you find. It is important to see what you are up against as well as use what they have learned to your advantage.

Chances are, your customers have grown accustomed to the structure and navigation of your competitors' Spanish websites. In essence, you keep the things that work and scrap the things that do not. After all, why reinvent the wheel when you can just make it rounder?

Look & Feel

The style, images and colors of your website should be selected with one goal in mind: getting your visitors to take action or remember your brand. Your visitors must be able to relate to the look and feel of your site, not just the words. Spanish text is a great start, but truly successful Generation Equis marketing requires a website with the style, colors and images that appeal to the demographic.

But be careful: Generation Equis is a culturally diverse group. Your job is to appeal to the commonalties that they share, while avoiding stereotypes or isolating one part of the demographic to focus on another.

For example, using an image of a Hispanic male or female on your site would be considered culturally acceptable by most members of Generation Equis. However, using images of the Mexican flag throughout your site would not only alienate consumers from Spanish speaking countries other than Mexico, but it may even be negatively perceived by first and second generation Spanish speakers in the United States who identify themselves as Americans, not Mexicans.

Reflect for a moment on how many Fortune 500 websites you have seen that use a small Mexican flag symbol as the primary means of accessing the Spanish version of their website. How do you think someone originally from Argentina, Columbia or Spain would respond to that?

Now consider how many English websites for companies in the United States you have seen that have a red, white and blue color scheme with American flags all over them. Not many. The goal is to have your site appeal to Generation Equis by reflecting their culture with subtle style, image and color variations that they can identify with—just as you would with any target audience.

Content is Key

Once you have the structure, navigation, style, images and colors of your site planned out, it is time to think about content. The competitive intelligence you have collected is a great place to start—see what kind of content others targeting Generation Equis are using.

If budget allows, you may want to consider focus groups or market research studies of current and potential customers who fall into the Generation Equis demographic. Find out what they need, what they would like from your company, and what they would love to have incorporated into your Spanish website.

Consider both the "what" and the "why" of the content you will have on your website. Be rigorous in deciding what to include and what to leave out. A detailed content strategy will help you build a focused and effective site that both appeals to your users and gets the business results you want.

Your Product and Services Offering

In addition to identifying the content you will be placing on your website, analyze your products or services and confirm whether Generation Equis will be attracted to the same offering you present to mainstream consumers. You may need to modify your existing offerings to include new products or services attractive to Generation Equis consumers and drive incremental sales from this untapped market.

Once you have a website development plan together, revisit the goals of your site and make sure your plan is a roadmap to achieving those goals.

Whether you are looking to use your site to brand your company to Generation Equis, sell a product or service, or even create a call to action for your traditional marketing channels, you need to confirm that your site will ultimately include all the necessary tools and functions to achieve your goals.

A GRINGO'S GUIDE TO ONLINE HISPANIC MARKETING

CHAPTER THREE

METRICS & REPORTING

"Generation Equis – can explode your growth; celebrate your results"

You cannot determine success or failure of any of your online business activities if you do not track and measure their effectiveness. Just like a traditional brick and mortar business, your online business must also identify key metrics, establish goals, implement standardized reporting and track your results.

Do not start any marketing effort unless you put the tools in place to accurately monitor and evaluate the results of the specific marketing approach you try. The data and information you gather will be essential in measuring and managing your online business and marketing campaigns.

It is hard to find your way to success when you do not know where you have been, how you got there, or what adjustments you can make to improve your results.

The key strategies to consider while implementing metrics and reporting are:

• **Traffic:** Just like monitoring traditional brick and mortar business traffic, you need to track how many unique and return visitors are coming to your site. You need to attract consistent and growing traffic to your website so you can widen the top of the conversion funnel – the more customers you get in, the more you can ultimately convert.

• **Content:** Which pages are users visiting on your site? Which pages are most popular or unpopular and why? Which pages have the highest bounce rates? Find out which pages work and use that knowledge to refine your website and improve your site's effectiveness.

• **Sources:** Are your visitors coming from search engines? Banner advertisements? Links from other website? What keywords do visitors use to find your site? You can monitor the effectiveness of your marketing efforts by closely tracking the sources of your traffic.

• **Conversions:** How many visitors are converting or enabling you to achieve the objectives of the site? If the goal of the site is to sell a product, how many visitors do you receive before you make a sale?

This is just the beginning of what you can learn from a solid analytics program and by reviewing your web logs. Depending on the nature of your business, you may also want to know:

- The geographic distribution of your visitors.

- The Internet connection and browser your visitors use.

- The exit pages where visitors leave your site.

- How many customers you lose during the checkout process.

Analytics and web logs are a great way to identify what is working and what is not. If you notice that a lot of visitors are going through check-out and not ordering, most likely there is an issue with your checkout process. Perhaps excessive shipping rates are stopping visitors from completing the purchase. Without the analytics data, you will not even know where to look.

If you find a page that is getting visitors from search engines when people search for a certain popular Spanish search string, do the same search and see where your site appears in the results. You may then want to optimize that page of your website further to increase your position in search results for that term, or retain your high ranking.

If you notice a lot of traffic from a website where you are running banners or a specific Spanish PPC keyword then it may be worth boosting your advertising budget for those tactics.

You may also find that you are getting a lot of traffic from a certain source but that traffic is not converting to meet your goals. This could be a signal for you to limit or phase out marketing to that source. You cannot measure results without tracking your progress.

Whether you use free web based programs like Google Analytics, shown in **Figure 3.1**, which allows you to set-up automated daily report delivery via email and facilitates custom reporting, or you

use a paid analytics program like VisiStat, shown in **Figure 3.2**, it
is important that you monitor your web traffic.

Figure 3.1: Free Analytics Program – Google Analytics

Source: www.google.com/analytics

Figure 3.2: Paid Analytics Program – VisiStat

Source: www.visistat.com

A GRINGO'S GUIDE TO ONLINE HISPANIC MARKETING

CHAPTER FOUR

SEARCH ENGINE OPTIMIZATION

"Generation Equis – can they find your website?"

S earch engine optimization is most effectively implemented during the initial design phase of a website, BEFORE you go into production. It is much more difficult to optimize an existing website for the search engines than it is to optimize a new website to be search engine friendly.

Since starting from scratch is the best way to go with your Spanish (Generation Equis targeted) website, you will be in a good position to have search engine optimization planned and implemented from the beginning.

Keep in mind that close to ten percent of all online searches in the United States are conducted in Spanish, while less than one company out of fifty-thousand has listed their keywords in Spanish.

Does this sound like an opportunity? English and Spanish search engines offer free targeted organic traffic so an Internet user can easily find what they are looking for. In most cases, the longer your website is listed with a search engine, the better placement your website will receive in search results. Better placement results in more visitors!

Best of all, with the right planning and search engine optimization visitors will find your website first. Why? Because your website is at the top of the search engine results. That translates directly to more visitors. How often do you go to page 2 or 3 of your web search results to find what you are looking for? Not likely very often, unless you are looking for your own website.

The key strategies to consider while optimizing your website for the search engines are:

• **Web Crawler Friendly Design:** Just like targeting the general Internet population, your Generation Equis site still needs to have the same crawl-friendly design of a traditional website; you still need an error free site, a robots.txt file and an XML sitemap.

• **Using Keywords:** Your domain name, tags, links, images and content must be keyword rich with both English and Spanish keywords that will attract Generation Equis visitors to your site. You must also consider culturally significant keywords such as; Hispanic, Latino and Latina as well as accents as they will truly set you apart from other Spanish websites.

• **Search Engine Submission:** Manual submission to the major English search engines and directories will help drive traffic to your website. It is imperative that you submit your site to the Spanish search engines as well. Finally, keep in mind that the major English websites such as Google, MSN, Lycos and Alta Vista also have Spanish websites that require a separate submission for your Spanish site.

Now let's go into more detail about each of these topics.

Web Crawler Friendly Design

The first step in the search engine optimization process is ensuring that your web developer builds a search engine friendly website.

Similar to a traditional English website, your Spanish website should be built free of coding errors, contain a robots.txt file and an XML sitemap. If the search engines cannot fully access your website due to design or implementation errors, you will be penalized by the search engines with a lower ranking in the search results, or no ranking at all—which means fewer visitors to your website. If Generation Equis is not able to locate your pages, what is the point of investing time and money in search engine optimization?

There are ample tools available to validate HTML or scripting as well as tools and programs that will verify your robots.txt file. HTML or scripting languages such as PHP are the programming languages used to build most websites. A Robots.txt file is a simple text file in your main web directory that generally has a link to your sitemap so the search engines can find it and it also tells the search engines which website pages that they should or should not index and present to the public.

An XML sitemap is an index of all of the individual pages contained in your website that assists the search engines in indexing your site's content. There are plenty of programs available that will create an XML sitemap and even update your sitemap automatically hourly, daily, and weekly, etc. to reflect any changes to your site.

After setting up your sitemap, your developer should also set up a "cron job" that will ping, or notify, the major search engines each time that your sitemap is updated so they can return and re-index your site to reflect any recent changes.

Using Keywords

Have you ever searched for something on a major search engine like Google, Yahoo or Bing and noticed that there were millions of websites that matched the terms that you searched for? Although Generation Equis has migrated to the Internet in a similar fashion as mainstream America has, most of Corporate America is still struggling to reach out to Generation Equis online. This means online marketing to Hispanics is currently a less competitive, and almost untapped market, wide open for the taking!

Corporate America, and top Internet marketers, may have a monopoly on the majority of the common English keywords with the major English search engines. They are most often listed on the first page of those millions of pages of results that are returned for any given search string. Spanish keywords and Spanish search engines are still wide open for the taking. Not only are Spanish keywords used less often on the web, thereby giving you an opportunity to receive good Search Engine Results Placement (SERP), but they are often erroneously used due to poor translations of English to Spanish, special characters and accents.

Keywords are the single words or phrases people would use most often when searching the major search engines for your business, product, or service. It is believed that a big component of the secret algorithm that search engines use when indexing your site and deciding where to rank your website in search results is your domain name.

Some people ask what is so important about a domain name. Many of our English website clients have told us that they thought if you register the shortest, catchiest domain name or have your company's name in your web address that you do not have to market your website and the sales will start trickling in.

We have also had people tell us that they have heard about the seven figure plus price tags that the sale of domains like Drugs.com and CreditCard.com brought in so they want to register a bunch of short and catchy domain names and just sell them in a few years for millions and retire.

The truth is that the very few high yielding domains that sold for millions of dollars were initially registered decades ago by early adopters to the Internet. A few years back, pre-recession, we remember more than a few neighbors making six and in some cases seven figure profits off of houses they bought only ten years ago. Recent events have proved that those days are over. As far as short and catchy English domains go, good luck finding one and even if you do, you will still need to market your website. Contrary to what you may hear some people say, website visitors do not just appear out of nowhere.

Finding a good domain name for your Spanish site is easier, mostly because Corporate America has not jumped on the Spanish web development bandwagon yet and neither have most of the domain name speculators (AKA squatters) or web developers. Your focus on Generation Equis should allow you to register a short and catchy Spanish domain that you may even be able to make a little money off of someday when the majority of Corporate America jumps on the Generation Equis bandwagon.

Adding your company's name to your website really depends on the nature of your business and the goals of your website. In some cases you need to use your company name in your website domain so your current customers can find you and you can protect your brand.

However, if you are using the Internet to drive incremental sales by marketing to new customers and prospects, they may not be looking for your company by name., If they are going to search for a website with your company name in it, they are probably not new customers, unless they became familiar with your company through advertising.

We generally tell customers that the key to finding a great domain is identifying an available domain that is rich in keywords related to their product or service. If you don't need to brand your company by using a web address with your company name in it, use a keyword rich domain that will help with your placement in search results. Plus, new customers can associate these keywords with your products or services.

Using effective keywords during the design of your site is also critical to search engine optimization. The first step in using effective keywords is keyword research. This is where your bilingual web developer, a bilingual employee or a bilingual friend can really be an asset. You need to create a list of potential keywords a customer would use to search for your company or products, so they can be translated into Spanish.

Assuming that you have an English website, start with the English keywords that have been successful for you and have them properly translated to Spanish. Of course, only translate the keywords if the Spanish versions would still apply to your business and would be used by Generation Equis when searching for a product or service like yours.

Keep in mind that any, and all, translations have to be done by a *fully bilingual* person. Have you ever used an online translation program to translate something from a foreign language to

English only to find that the translation makes no sense at all? You had a better contextual understanding looking at the picture above the foreign language text than you did when the translator software, or program, that you used translated it into English.

Translation is just another opportunity for you to set your company apart in your search engine placement. It is likely that some of your competitors made the mistake of improperly translating keywords during the translation process, giving your website a great chance to rank higher in the search engines' results.

This is a terrific opportunity to gain some competitive intelligence and get ideas for your own keywords. Take a look at your competitors' websites. By right clicking on your competitor's site and selecting the "view source" option, you will be able to see the keywords they are using in their meta-tags and description tag. Obviously, you do not want to directly copy their keywords and you never want to use their company name, brand or other keyword that may be protected under intellectual property laws. The idea here is simply to help generate ideas for your list of potential keywords list by giving you some keyword ideas to expand on.

Sit down with your bilingual web developer, employee or friend and brainstorm all of the words, or sets of words, that you think your customers would use when searching for your products as well as breaking out a thesaurus and looking up applicable synonyms. Then add their culturally and grammatically correct translations to your potential keyword list.

Do not hesitate to also add English keywords to your list of potential keywords. Make sure they are culturally relevant such as: "Hispanic," "bilingual," and "Latina," and are commonly used by members of Generation Equis. Stay away from using English keywords like "Spanish" or "Spanish shoes," as most Spanish speakers searching for a Spanish website would use the word Espanol, or Español, in their search, not "Spanish."

If someone searches for, "Spanish shoes," they are most likely looking to buy shoes from Spain on an English website versus searching for a Spanish site that sells shoes or "zapatos" in Spanish.

The Spanish language uses accent marks and special characters in some words, but not all keyboards support using these accents and special characters. It is important to consider adding both versions of Spanish words, with and without the accent, to your list of potential keywords. Proper use of accents may also get your website to the first page of results in the search engines, so mind your P's and Q's–or rather mind your ñ's and Ñ's.

Now that you have compiled a list of potential keywords, it is time to research their popularity. Their popularity will tell you how often your keywords are searched for in a given time period so you can identify the more popular keywords and keyword combinations.

This can be done in a couple of ways. First, you can enter the keywords into the major English and Spanish search engines and see how many, what type and which of your competitors' sites come up in the results. However, it is often more effective to use a tool specifically designed for measuring keyword popularity. We recommend using Google Suggest, Overture, or Wordtracker to measure the popularity of your keywords. Be sure to rank each keyword on your list by popularity and keep the forty highest ranked keywords at the top of your list while retaining the others for future campaigns.

With your ranked keyword list in hand, it is now time to sit down with the web developer and plan out the keyword placement for your site. Start by selecting your top ten ranked keywords to optimize your homepage. When using keywords to optimize a webpage, you should focus on keyword density in your tags, headings, links, image alt tags, and content while avoiding excessive repetition. A good rule of thumb: if it makes sense when you read it or it is in context, it is not too excessive.

Meta-tags provide information about a given web page, most often to help search engines categorize them correctly. They are hidden in the source code of the web page, do not affect how the page is displayed and are not visible to visitors unless they view the source code of your web page. Meta-tags allow you to insert keywords into the title, description and keywords of your page so they will be indexed by the search engines.

In addition to meta-tags, the alt tags of your web page can be a great place to insert your keywords. Alt tags were developed to present text to visitors when an image does not load and to provide a textual description of an image. Alt tags are somewhat hidden to visitors unless they mouse over the images they are attached to. Some screen reading software for vision-impaired users will also read the alt tags attached to images, to help these users understand what is on the page.

Links are also a great location for your keywords. Whether the links are outbound, to other websites, or inbound, to other pages in your website, try to use your keywords if possible when creating your links. This creates relevance in the eyes of the search engines and increases your rank in search results.

In addition to links, your image files can be a great place to use your keywords. Instead of naming your images logo.jpg or button.jpg, try inserting your keywords into your filename. For example our site logo is named GenerationEquisMedia.jpg versus logo.jpg.

This strategy not only gives you better keyword density on your web page, it also optimizes your page for the "image search" that a lot of the major search engines offer. Remember, the bots that search engines send to crawl your site can't "read" images, Flash files, videos or other non-text content. If you do not tag these assets with relevant keywords, the search engines will simply ignore them and you will lose the potential SEO value they can provide.

Content and text are another great venue for keyword placement. The challenge is providing keyword rich text and content without distracting the user. If your text and content is written with your keywords in mind, it will only help with your placement in the search engine results. Just be careful not to go too far – always write for readability first. If you are creating content that is relevant to your customers, it should naturally contain the right keywords.

Finally, keep in mind that search engines place greater value on keywords in the large headings and bolded print of your text and content.

Once you have planned how to optimize your homepage, select the other main pages of your site and plan on using three different keywords from your top ten ranked keywords list to optimize each page. Repeat this process, page by page, using keywords from the remaining top forty ranked keywords list.

The goal is to optimize each page of your site for different keywords, thereby increasing the chances of one of your pages being found no matter which of your keywords is searched for.

Search Engine Submission

There are a couple of basic methods you can use to submit your site to the major search engines. You can either submit the home, or index page, of your website or you can submit your XML sitemap. Either way, you need to decide whether you are going to automatically submit your site to the search engines or do so manually.

We always recommend manual submission as it is often better received by the search engines and can give you additional drill-down or category information that is not available with automated submission.

Although Generation Equis uses the major English search engines such as Google (**Figure 4.2**), Yahoo (**Figure 4.3**) and MSN (**Figure 4.4**), they also utilize Spanish search engines as well as Spanish versions of the major English search engines.

You cannot stop at just submitting your Spanish site to the major search engines, you also need to submit your site to the Spanish version of the mainstream English search engines such as the Spanish version of Google (**Figure 4.5**), Yahoo (**Figure 4.6**) and MSN (**Figure 4.7**).

Figure 4.2: Google Search Engine – English Version

Source: www.google.com

Figure 4.3: Yahoo Search Engine – English Version

Source: www.yahoo.com

Figure 4.4: MSN Search Engine – English Version

Source: www.msn.com

Figure 4.5: Google Search Engine – Spanish Version

A GRINGO'S GUIDE TO ONLINE HISPANIC MARKETING

Figure 4.6: Yahoo Search Engine – Spanish Version

Figure 4.7: MSN Search Engine – Spanish Version

A GRINGO'S GUIDE TO ONLINE HISPANIC MARKETING

Source: latino.msn.com

It is also imperative that you submit your website to the Spanish specific search engines such as; Terra (**Figure 4.8**), Mexico Global (**Figure 4.9**) and Univision (**Figure 4.10**).

To properly submit your website to the Spanish specific search engines, you will need a text file with the following information, in Spanish, available to copy and paste into the submission fields:

- Title: The title of your website.

- Description: The description of your website that you want to appear on the search engine results page.

- Categories: Two relevant categories that apply to your website.

- Email: An email account that you are open to receiving spam email in. It is not a good idea to use your regular email address.

Figure 4.8: Terra – Spanish Search Engine

Source: www.terra.com

Figure 4.9: Mexico Global – Spanish Search Engine

Source: www.mexicoglobal.com

A GRINGO'S GUIDE TO ONLINE HISPANIC MARKETING

Figure 4.10: Univision – Spanish Search Engine

Source: www.univision.com

Directories are another way to freely market and promote your site to Generation Equis as well as build quality inbound links to your site that the search engines recognize and reward you for.

Submitting your site to the Spanish directories such as Hispanic Surf (**Figure 4.11**), Top 100 Latino (**Figure 4.11**) and Busca Pique (**Figure 4.13**) is another important way to optimize your website for search engines.

Directory submissions often require a manual submission as well as a complete description so it is important that your bilingual web developer, employee or friend completes the submission on your behalf.

A GRINGO'S GUIDE TO ONLINE HISPANIC MARKETING

Figure 4.11: Hispanic Surf – Spanish Directory

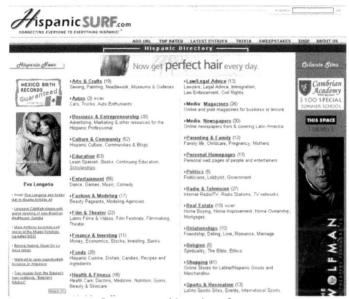

Source: www.hispanicsurf.com

Figure 4.12: Top 100 Latino – Spanish Directory

Source: www.top100latino.com

Figure 4.13: Busca Pique – Spanish Directory

A GRINGO'S GUIDE TO ONLINE HISPANIC MARKETING

Source: www.buscapique.com

CHAPTER FIVE

ONLINE MESSAGING

"Generation Equis – are you speaking their language?"

Whether you are messaging to the visitors on your website via email or with opt-in methods such as newsletters, it is important to track their preferences and "speak their language." For example, if a visitor signs up for a newsletter on your Spanish website, they will expect it to be delivered to them in Spanish and have it contain content relevant to both Generation Equis and your company's offering.

In many cases, online messaging can be automated. For example, you can build your website to send automatic purchase orders by email when a customer places an order, or deliver automated responses to customer inquiries, etc.

It is very important that you take the time to plan your online messaging system and use the correct tools to implement it before you launch. If it is done properly in the beginning, it should be on auto-pilot and serve you well—and save you the time and expense of correcting the system later.

The key strategies to consider while developing your online messaging systems are:

•   **Email:** Your email relationship with your customers and prospects is much like a normal offline relationship in many respects. One key requirement of maintaining a good relationship with consumers in the real world is getting their attention, staying in touch, personalizing your message and interactive communication.

•   **Electronic Newsletters:** Electronic newsletters are a great way to stay in touch with, and provide value to, customers and prospects. They are gaining in popularity, and for good reason. With electronic newsletters, there are no printing or mailing costs involved and they can usually be published for a fraction of the cost, and in a fraction of the time, of traditional printed newsletters.

Additionally, because online newsletters can be instantly delivered to readers throughout the world at the click of a button, these publications are ideal for communicating timely information to readers.

Let's explore these two powerful communications tools in greater detail.

Email

Email can be a powerful brand and relationship-building tool for your business. Sending a branded invoice, thank you email, press release on your company, new product notification or even a relevant article to a customer or prospect who has opted in or made a purchase on your website can help build customer loyalty and set your company apart from your competitors.

In order to communicate with Generation Equis via email messaging, you need to ensure that your email is opened, read and understood.

A properly composed email message contains:

Concise subject lines — Try to keep your subject lines to 35 characters or less. E-mail clients like Outlook and Eudora and webmail providers like Gmail, Hotmail and Yahoo frequently truncate subject lines at approximately 35 characters and so do the majority of mobile email or cell phone clients.

Personalization — It is important to use your customer's name in the greeting of the email and use a personal, or team name, in the signature, i.e. Mr. Jones or The XYZ Customer Support Team.

Top billed content — It is highly likely the user will not even bother scrolling down to read your message, unless you use content that will catch their eye at the top of the message.

Language — If the recipient of your email is being contacted due to an opt-in or action on a Spanish website, your email should be in Spanish. If the recipient of your email is being contacted due to an opt-in or action on an English website, your email should be in English. You should also give them the option, and information necessary, to contact you directly in their preferred language.

Electronic Newsletters

Because online newsletters can be instantly delivered to readers at the click of a button, these publications are ideal for communicating timely information to readers.

A properly composed electronic newsletter affords:

Cost-effectiveness

Electronic newsletters are much less expensive than designing and printing traditional newsletters and the postage or delivery expense associated with sending traditional newsletters.

Wider Reach

With your own electronic newsletter, you can reach millions of customers or prospects instantaneously—and advertise your products or services on a regular basis—for free.

Targeting

Electronic newsletters allow you to encourage opt-ins from your visitors, determine their subjects of interest and focus on specific interests that they may have.

Electronic Newsletters for Generation Equis require:

Targeted Content

Items of interest — Choose news or information that is interesting to Generation Equis, yet in line with your business goals. Include general topics as well as specific items which they would find appealing. Bookmark or monitor RSS feeds or use a newsfeed service to collect this type of data.

Guidance/Tips — Offer tips and advice. Generation Equis readers are naturally drawn to any article with "How to" in the title if it is useful. Tap the knowledge within your company such as front line members, your management team or even C-level Generation Equis employees.

Lists — Whenever possible, use lists—particularly numbered lists—to attract readers. Use titles like "5 Ways to..." or "6 Tips for..." Readers like to know they are only making a small commitment of time. Lists are a proven method to attract them to click and engage with your content.

Interactivity — Make it interactive. Include a quick poll relating to an industry topic. It should be a topic of interest to Generation Equis. People love to speak out, even if only through a quick vote, and see how their peers view an issue.

User-Friendly Format

KISS – The popular KISS theory, or **K**eep **I**t **S**imple **S**tupid, applies here. Keep the body of the newsletter short by providing headlines and excerpts linking to longer articles on your website. This will encourage your visitors to return to your site and increase traffic.

Give links to both the English and Spanish versions when possible. This enables readers to scan the content quickly and then click on the link to articles of interest – in the language that they prefer.

Title - Include your newsletter title at the beginning of the subject field. This will help the reader differentiate your newsletter from junk emails. It will also allow them to filter your newsletter into a separate folder with the use of email filters.

Readability - Provide both HTML and plain text versions. Format it with hard line breaks at sixty-five characters per line. This is a good practice because proper spacing enables the majority of your readers to see your message in the format that you intended it to be viewed. It is also considered to be more viewer friendly when you follow this guideline. An easy way to implement this is with a text editor. Configure it to insert hard carriage returns at the end of each sixty-five character line.

A GRINGO'S GUIDE TO ONLINE HISPANIC MARKETING

CHAPTER SIX

INTERNET MARKETING

"Generation Equis – they are anxious to meet you, introduce yourself!"

The Internet has grown up. It is not the same as it was before the dot-com bubble burst. In those days, scams were commonplace, and many people were making money for doing nothing. Today, the Internet has become a legitimate and viable channel for reputable companies to do business.

The beauty of the Internet today is that any business, small or large, can compete fairly and the business with the best skills and planning will win. In short, it is like any other mature business channel, with its own rules and strategies for success.

If you experiment with the different approaches in this section, you will find which works the best for your business. As with any marketing campaign, proceed with caution.

Start slow, evaluate the results, then ramp up the approach that is the most cost effective and yields the results you are looking for. When you see the desired return on your marketing investment, increase your investment in that area. Then monitor the results and repeat the cycle.

Internet Marketing Options

First, let's explore the many online marketing options available that are not targeted to Generation Equis, but to all Internet users. Then, we will give you specific information on how to execute a targeted marketing plan for Generation Equis online.

Do not start any marketing effort unless you can accurately monitor and evaluate the results of the specific approach you try.

Please review the Metrics & Reporting chapter of this book for the information you need to proceed – the right way.

The concepts are the same. The important differences are how you message (the text and visual presentation) and which online channels you use.

Affiliate Programs

Affiliate programs allow you to sign up resellers, or advertisers, of your products and services and have them earn a commission, or referral fee, for the sales that they generate or the visitors that they send to your website.

The key considerations when launching an online affiliate program are:

- Determining whether you are going to launch your own affiliate program or use the services of an affiliate network such as Commission Junction (**Figure 6.1**), LinkShare (**Figure 6.2**) or Click Bank (**Figure 6.3**).

- Determining the commission, or referral bonus, structure you will offer to your affiliates. It is important that you offer a competitive payout that will motivate your affiliates to promote your website versus that of your competition.

- Indentifying how you are going to track traffic, sales, and commissions as well as how you are going to deliver this information and payments to your affiliates. When you use an affiliate network, they will manage this part of the affiliate program for you.

- Developing an affiliate marketing area with sales tools such as banners, text and product images that your affiliates can download and use to promote your website and sell your products.

- Creating policies governing the terms of your affiliate program that your affiliates must accept to participate, and procedures to avoid Click Fraud. When you use an affiliate network, they will manage this part of the affiliate program for you.

- Just like a new website, your affiliate program will need to be promoted and advertised to potential affiliates.

When using affiliate programs to do business online with Generation Equis, it is important for you to provide all of your materials in Spanish and focus on bringing in affiliates with Spanish websites. Examples of this would be Spanish:

- Policies, terms and conditions.

- Affiliate website, newsletters and emails.

- Banners, text and product images.

- Affiliate advertising and marketing.

Figure 6.1: Commission Junction – Affiliate Program

Source: www.commissionjunction.com

Figure 6.2: LinkShare – Affiliate Program

Source: www.linkshare.com

Figure 6.3: Click Bank – Affiliate Program

Source: www.clickbank.com

A GRINGO'S GUIDE TO ONLINE HISPANIC MARKETING

Banner Advertising

Larger websites, online newspapers, search engines and even some blogs offer space on their website for banner ads which are graphical display advertisements that link to other websites.

Placing banner ads on other websites that link to your website will drive immediate traffic to your website. This translates into sales, strengthens your brand online and in some cases the banner ads can even be counted as inbound links that improve your placement on the search engine results page.

The key considerations to effectively utilize banner advertising campaigns are:

- Establish a banner advertising budget, your targeted return on investment, or conversion percentage, and determine the websites where you would like to see your banner ads displayed.

- Design marketing-focused banners, in all of the traditional sizes, which are product or service specific and determine which pages of your website each banner should link to.

- Create a banner advertising marketing plan that combines paid banner advertising and banner exchanges with other websites.

Before launching a banner advertising campaign, familiarize yourself with the banner advertising vocabulary below:

- **Banner** – An ad image displayed on another website that links back to your site or a landing page for your product or service.

- **Hits** – The number of times that a specific webpage is visited.

- **Cookies** – Files stored by a computer or web browser, and passed to your website, used to identify users and their activities online.

- **Impressions** – The amount of times a banner has been seen.

- **Cost per Mille (CPM)** – Cost per thousand impressions.

- **Run of Network (RON)** – A cost effective banner ad buying option in which an ad may appear on any page of the target network or website.

- **Clicks** – The amount of visits you receive from a banner.

- **Click Through Rate (CTR)** – Percentage of clicks received versus total impressions.

- **Conversions** – The percentage of visitors who ultimately make a purchase after clicking through a banner to your website, or who otherwise fulfill your goal or respond favorably to your call to action.

When using banner advertising to do business online with Generation Equis, it is important that you design your banners with the same principles in mind as when you are developing a

Spanish website. Your banner content, look and feel, and offer should be designed to appeal to Generation Equis.

When considering where to place your banners, only choose banner exchanges that target other Spanish websites. Just as you do not want to display English banners on your Spanish website nor do you want your Spanish banners to be displayed on English websites.

When purchasing banner advertisements, you will most likely see a better Return on Investment (ROI) if you purchase banners from larger Spanish websites whose visitors not only speak Spanish but could benefit from your business offering such as Soy Entrepreneur (**Figure 6.4**) or Univision (**Figure 6.5**).

Because Spanish online advertising is so targeted, it is often less expensive than traditional online advertising.

Figure 6.4: Soy Entrepreneur – Spanish Banner Host

Source: www.soyentrepreneur.com/contenidos/anuncie_aqui.html

Figure 6.5: Univision – Spanish Banner Host

Source: www.univisionpartnergroup.com/espanol

A GRINGO'S GUIDE TO ONLINE HISPANIC MARKETING

Pay-Per-Click (PPC) – Google & Yahoo

Pay-Per-Click, or PPC, advertising is an online advertising model whereby advertisers pay the site hosting their advertisement only when their ad is clicked and they receive a hit, or actual visit, to their website.

PPC search engine advertising typically involves advertisers bidding on keyword phrases relevant to their product, service or offering, versus content websites that generally charge a fixed price per click but are usually less targeted.

The key considerations to effectively utilize PPC advertising campaigns are:

- Keyword selection can make or break your PPC campaign. Similar to search engine optimization, when planning your PPC advertising campaign you need to determine the keywords that accurately describe your business, your product and what you offer. The keywords you choose are matched to users who are searching on those terms. The correct keywords will attract visitors who convert.

- Establish a budget for your PPC campaign whether prepaid or pay-as-you-go. In addition to the overall campaign budget, you need to set a minimum and maximum budget for each and every keyword or phrase that you plan to advertise.

- An effective PPC advertisement will have a catchy title and text description that will pull the viewers attention away from the organic, or free, search engine results and draw them to your advertisement. Keep in mind that you will be charged for each click on your advertisement. Therefore, what draws people to click is extremely important. Typically, people will click on something that has a catchy title and description that applies to what they are interested in and searching for.

- Make sure when they click on your ad that visitors find what your ad implied. "Bait and switch" will not work with today's savvy online shoppers, and would be a bad business decision, since you are paying for every click. Your page and the product or service it markets should be related to what enticed the users to click on your ad in the first place. This way, you are far more likely to bring quality visitors to your website who find just what they were looking for. When you are paying for each and every visitor, as you do with a PPC advertising campaign, quality is better than quantity.

- PPC advertising channels are a dime a dozen and click fraud, or fake hits that advertisers are charged for, have given the PPC advertising industry a black eye in recent years. It is generally safer, to avoid fraud, to use the big PPC advertisers such as; Google AdWords (**Figure 6.6**) and Yahoo Search Marketing (**Figure 6.7**).

Figure 6.6: Google AdWords – PPC advertising host

Source: www.adwords.com

Figure 6.7: Yahoo Search Marketing – PPC advertising host

Source: advertising.yahoo.com/smallbusiness

Forums and Groups

Groups and forums are the online home away from home of people with similar interests.

A good forum has loyal members that build friendships, share information and learn from other members. Most importantly, they check in, or log in, daily and love to socialize with other members.

Groups and forums can be excellent marketing resources when used properly and are considered a secret marketing channel by many Internet marketing professionals.

The key considerations and benefits of targeted group and forum marketing are:

- **Knowledge** – By participating in groups and forums, you will learn about the interests, likes and dislikes of the members – your target market – and it will help you grow your online business.

- **Content** – When you find yourself in need of content, you can always start a discussion on a subject in a group or forum and receive suggestions directly from members of the market that you are targeting.

- **Marketing** – After you become an active member of a group or forum and have a few relevant posts and discussions under your belt, you can add a link to your website to your signature and profile page. If your posts are good, and on topic, they will be read and people will click on your website out of curiosity.

  A word of caution: If your posts are only related to your product or service and do not provide any real value to the conversation, you will be ignored (or worse) by the community. Be sure you are contributing value to the conversation and people will be naturally interested in visiting your site.

- **SEO Friendly** – In a lot of cases, search engines recognize the inbound links to your website contained in the signature of your group and forum posts and this can help increase your ranking with the search engines.

Group and forum members love to talk, and share information, via group or forum posts. If you are able to join groups or forums and speak at their level, on the topics they're interested in, they will roll out the red carpet and you will be invited into their online community. Once you are invited in, you want them to enjoy your company and be happy that they extended you an invitation. That means contributing value and not using the forum as a platform to sell. That is the best way to ensure that you will be welcome in the future and will not be called out, or flagged, and will not get kicked out, or banned.

Some of the biggest mistakes that Internet marketers make when utilizing groups or forums to promote their websites are:

- Using the forum to blatantly advertise their website by posting information about it in or placing a link to their website in their post.

- Adding a link to their website to their profile page or signature as soon as they join without establishing a reputation as a true contributor to the forum.

- Private messaging other members and promoting their website.

- In essence the biggest mistake of all; SPAMMING, SPAMMING & more SPAMMING.

Those tactics will get your post flagged and removed before you can refresh your screen and you can even be banned for life from that community. In the case of a moderated forum, your post will most likely not even be seen by any of its members. Why? A good moderator can see through spam in a heartbeat and will delete your post before it is even visible to other community members.

When using groups and forums to promote your website to Generation Equis, you must select the groups and forums centered on a common interest that is equally of interest to Generation Equis, your customers and the potential customers you are targeting.

It is equally important that you select high-traffic, Spanish groups and forums that are well ranked with the search engines such as; Terra (**Figure 6.9**), Yahoo Grupos (**Figure 6.10**) and Hispavista (**Figure 6.11**).

Figure 6.9: Terra Foros – Spanish Forums

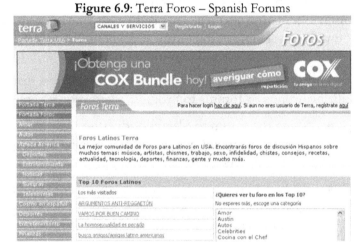

Source: forums.terra.com/forums

A GRINGO'S GUIDE TO ONLINE HISPANIC MARKETING

Figure 6.10: Yahoo Grupos – Spanish Group

Source: espanol.groups.yahoo.com

Figure 6.11: Hispavista Foros – Spanish Forum

Source: foros.hispavista.com

A GRINGO'S GUIDE TO ONLINE HISPANIC MARKETING

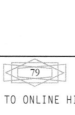

CHAPTER SEVEN

SOCIAL NETWORKING

"Generation Equis – they love to socialize; do you?"

It is hard to miss the social media craze that has swept through the mainstream Internet. Generation Equis is taking advantage of both the Spanish version of English websites such as MySpace, Facebook and LinkedIn as well as Spanish-only social media websites such as Sonico and Tuenti. In today's world, an online community presence is just as important to the success of your business as a physical community presence is.

Love them or hate them, social networks are here to stay. They will, however, continue to evolve and your business must evolve with them. The early Bulletin Board Systems of the 1970s and 1980s have evolved into sophisticated communities of today. The most popular sites include MySpace, Facebook, LinkedIn, YouTube, and Twitter. Lesser-known, but equally important Spanish social networking sites include Hi5, Sonico, and Tuenti. Literally hundreds of millions of people worldwide log into one or more of these networks daily and they must be included in your online strategy.

Goals for Social Networking

The goals to consider when developing your social networking plan are:

- Build your brand
- Increase loyalty
- Drive traffic to your website
- Buzz about being the "now" thing
- Be genuine
- Post relevant information to your business and the forum, blog or group you participate in

Social networking, when done correctly, can be one of the most cost effective marketing tools available, and it has long term benefits. There is a reason why Social Media degrees are offered at some universities. However, you should also understand that much of this can be self-taught. Just put on your sales hat.

Steps to Become a Social Success

Generation Equis came of age as the Internet was growing and most have had computers and Internet access since they were children. As such, they are not afraid of technology. They embrace it without any of the caution or concern of earlier generations and are willing to share a great deal more about themselves online. This can give you great insight into your prospective customers in a way that was previously only available through expensive market research.

Get started by creating your own blog or a group relevant to your business. Selling auto parts? Start a blog about restoring cars. Selling consulting services? Share some of your expertise online in your blog. Driving more traffic to your website from other highly ranked websites will improve your site's search engine ranking.

Encourage customers to leave reviews. Studies have shown that real customer reviews (good and bad) drive up conversion rates, because they are perceived by customers as more authentic than testimonials. Sharing the bad reviews shows customers that you have nothing to hide and stand behind your product or service. Done right, customer reviews are a much better investment than advertising that may or may not target who you are looking for.

The benefit of social networking is that you are able to control when and how you market to your customers. Once you have built a following, you can customize the message you send out based on your current business need. If sales are brisk, you would consider just a simple message promoting that you are a Spanish-friendly business. Likewise, if you needed a quick bump in your sales figures, you can send a special discount message directly to your customers.

The most active users on the social networking sites are very plugged into them. Often, they receive messages directly via text or email message on their cell phone the moment they are posted.

Social networks are essential to all businesses, but crucial to small businesses. With little if any out-of-pocket cost, small business owners can leverage social networks in promoting themselves and their businesses.

Be careful not to over use social networking sites. Sending too many messages will turn off your customers. Provide relevant information. Become part of the community and business type you are targeting. Send helpful links to interesting content, even if it is on someone else's site. If you have read a great article that relates to your area of expertise, share a link to it. The key is to

BE AUTHENTIC. The days of hyper-controlled, one-way conversations between a brand and its customers are over. If that is what you are after, it is best to avoid social networks entirely, because you will do more damage than good.

Participate in at least five forums, blogs, or groups daily. Be genuine. If you do not have the time to spend, then hire a professional to represent you. It will be marketing dollars well spent.

Social networking establishes credibility for you and your business. When done correctly, it can be like handing out millions of flyers every time you post relevant information to the forum, blog, or group you are active in. The other great advantage is that you will be driving very relevant traffic to your website. Not just traffic – the right traffic!

During your social endeavors, do not fear the negative or be timid. Always be respectful but post what you believe in. You are, after all, acting as an expert. Do your research to make sure that what you say is well founded. If you cause some conflict, that is ok. A little conflict is expected and often necessary for a healthy exchange of information and opinions. Just participate respectfully – don't make the mistake of talking down to your customers. Social networking has ushered in a new era of openness between businesses and customers. Participate authentically and you will be rewarded.

Introduction to Popular Social Sites

Now let's get more specific on how you can use Social Networking to benefit your business. In this section we will discuss the mainstream English websites. This should help give you the courage to get started. Once you start, and see the results, you will likely get hooked and not look at this as a chore but an important and satisfying part of your daily work regimen. After you master the English websites you will be ready to take advantage of the many Generation Equis-focused social sites. The same concepts will apply, but the audience is far more targeted.

Before you start signing up for the social sites, you should have a strategy in mind. An important first piece is your screen name. We recommend you create a unique user name that represents your business and another that represents you as an individual.

You can grow a following by applying the same user name across multiple social websites.. For example, if your business name is Technology Solutions you may use TechSolutionsOfHouston for your unique business name and your personal username may be JohnnyTheTechGuy. There is of course some room for creativity here. Keep in mind that many social networks, such as Twitter, impose character limits, so shorter is often better.

Take a day to look at what others are doing on the different sites you wish to participate in and you will get many ideas. Also, understand that you can create more than one personal account for different individuals who wish to represent your business. If you have multiple employees representing your business, it is a good idea to have some written guidelines in place. While you want them to be authentic, it is also important that they do not misrepresent your company. A good rule of thumb is to have employees explicitly state in their profiles that they work for your company, but that the views represented in their posts are their own.

The next important piece is your business strategy and goals for your social network. Come up with a short list of services your business provides and the type of people that may be interested in your business. A few captivating lines that summarize your business will also be helpful as you register on each site. Refer to this list as you explore each social website. This will help you participate in the right "social circles" that fit your business and goals.

Finally, we suggest that you come up with an email plan. We suggest using a unique email address for each social network that you join. This makes it much easier to manage your activities on each site.

Now let's look at some of the top social networking sites.

Figure 7.1: Social Networking Sites – Twitter

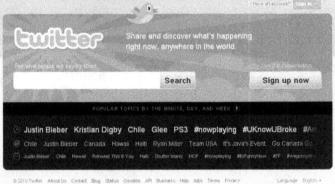

Source: www.twitter.com

Twitter (Figure 7.1) is a free service and ideal for:

- Spreading breaking news quickly – get the word out on current events, coupons/discounts, or anything related to your business.

- Enabling individuals to subscribe and receive instant updates on categories, news, and people that are of interest to them.

- Questions and Answers between peers or experts in a field.

To get started on Twitter:

A GRINGO'S GUIDE TO ONLINE HISPANIC MARKETING

1. Go to Twitter.com.

2. Search for your competitors to see how they are using the service. This will give you ideas how to use the service properly.

3. Register your business and personal user name(s).

4. Start Tweeting. Send messages about your business. Participate in areas that relate to your business strategy.

Twitter also provides a very useful overview of how to get started and explains the benefits of using their service. They appropriately call it Twitter101.

Figure 7.2: Social Networking Sites – Facebook

Source: www.facebook.com

Facebook (Figure 7.2) is a free service and ideal for:

- Making new friends.

- Keeping in contact with old friends and colleagues.

- Promoting your business to friends.

We consider Facebook to be more commonly used for pure social purposes as opposed to LinkedIn which is more focused on business and professional networking. Though do not underestimate it. With a few hundred million users and growing, you may be surprised at how many old friends will find you and friends of theirs that will be introduced to you. This is how you build your network.

The more people you know, the more people that can potentially benefit from what your business has to offer. After all, wouldn't you be more likely to buy a product or service based on a friend's recommendation or a referral from a friend of a friend?

To get started on Facebook:

1. Go to Facebook.com.

2. Search for your competitors to see how they are using the service. This will give you ideas how to use the service properly.

3. Register your business (create a business fan page).

4. Register your personal user name.

5. Be seen. Invite your friends to join you. Let them know what you are doing. Invite them to become "fans" of your business. It is a great way to hook up with old friends and colleagues as well as create new ones.

6. Send messages about your business. Write on your wall. Write on your friends' walls. Keep people informed about what you and your business are doing.

7. Participate in areas that relate to your business strategy.

Facebook also provides complete information on how to use their site. Simply visit Facebook.com and use their "Help"

feature. If you still have questions, the easiest way to learn is to ask a friend. That is a unique advantage of the site, you will find yourself quickly surrounded by friends who will gladly guide you through and give you tips on the best ways to use the service to achieve your goals.

Figure 7.4: Social Networking Sites – LinkedIn

Source: www.linkedin.com

LinkedIn (Figure 7.4) is one of the most popular online professional networking tools that we have found. It offers a free service for your personal use and a paid service for business use – currently starting at $24.95 a month. This is a small investment when you consider the exposure your business can get with this service. Even with the lowest priced package your business could be seen by over 60 million users.

We suggest you create a free personal and a business account. This way you build your personal credibility while also promoting your business.

A GRINGO'S GUIDE TO ONLINE HISPANIC MARKETING

LinkedIn is ideal for:

- Asking and answering questions – gain and share knowledge.

- Making new friends.

- Making new business contacts.

- Reconnecting with former colleagues.

- Promoting yourself to friends, colleagues, and others with similar areas of interest.

- Promoting your business to friends, colleagues, and others with similar areas of interest.

- Creating your own group that focuses on your business or any topic matter that you want to share with others.

- Selling products and services.

- Marketing research.

- Keeping informed and keeping others informed.

Be sure to complete all profile information. It is especially important to include your complete and accurate professional history. Once you do this you will be given the opportunity to connect with almost anybody who shares the same history as you. You can find people who went to the same schools or worked for the same companies that you did and they will be able to find you too.

To get started on LinkedIn:

1. Go to LinkedIn.com.

2. Complete your personal profile – use your full name.

3. Sign up to receive updates about those in your network.

4. Make your profile visible so that others can find you.

5. Build your network. Connect with those who share your past. Linked in will present you with people you may know every time you visit the website. When you recognize somebody, ask to connect with them.

6. Search for people from your past using the people search option.

7. Invite your friends from other networking sites to join you on LinkedIn.

8. Keep your profile current. Let everybody know what you are doing.

9. Create your own blog or group and actively post on a daily basis.

10. Ask and answer questions in your area of expertise. This builds credibility for yourself and those associated with you.

Once your personal profile is completed, set up a profile for the business you represent:

1. Go to LinkedIn.com.

2. Search for your competitors to see how they are using the service. This will give you ideas on how to best use the service to present the right image of your business and differentiate it from your competitors. You can use the business search option to find specific companies that are already active on LinkedIn.

3. Join and participate in industry groups that relate to your business.

4. Create a group, or multiple groups, that focus on topics related to your business. For example, if you represent a law firm specializing in business law, you may want to start a group that discusses current developments in law for the state you represent. The group name you select could be "California Law Discussions" with a purpose of "Keep up to date on the latest business laws that may impact your business."

5. Invite others to join and participate in your group. Raise relevant questions and answer questions that others raise. Keep your group alive with interesting topics.

6. Join multiple groups that relate to your business strategy.

7. Watch your business get traffic from your efforts.

Once you have set up your personal and business accounts and are comfortable using LinkedIn, you are ready to move forward with a focus on Generation Equis.

On July 23, 2008 LinkedIn added support for Spanish. Start a Spanish blog or group for your business or the business you represent. Let others know that you are a Generation Equis friendly business. Invite others that represent Generation Equis to join your network. You will be surprised at how quickly your network of individuals and other businesses will grow.

Figure 7.5: Social Networking Sites – YouTube

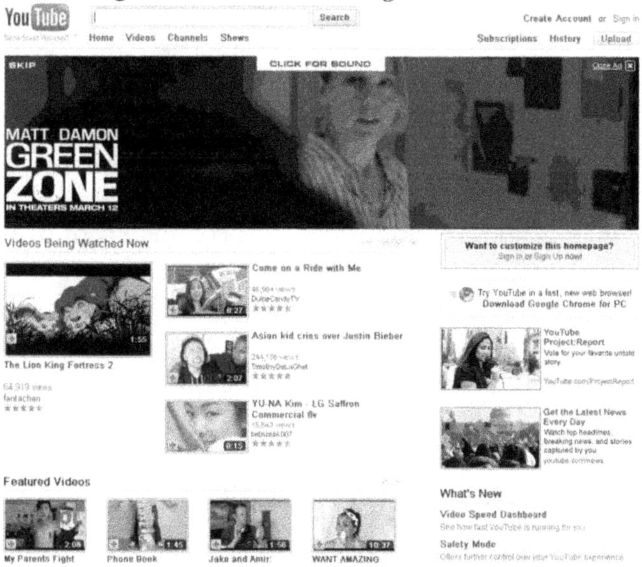

Source: www.youtube.com

YouTube (Figure 7.5) is widely used for entertainment but also can be a very effective business marketing tool. You can use it to show what makes your business different or better, display your products, and create a following of people who could become your customers. If you post the right video on YouTube, you will get immediate traffic to your website.

While marketing through YouTube may require a little more effort than other social networking approaches, the benefits can be well worth the investment. Your videos do not need to be professionally produced. Some businesses have found success using low-fidelity videos with their own employees as on-screen talent. Just like other social networking channels, YouTube offers an opportunity to build a deeper, more direct connection with your customers.

YouTube is a free service. You can post videos that promote your business and create a following by starting your own channel. And do not forget to link to your YouTube channel

A GRINGO'S GUIDE TO ONLINE HISPANIC MARKETING

from your traditional website as well as your Facebook and MySpace pages.

The most successful businesses on YouTube are those that upload a mix of videos that apply to their business. Some are just informative and some are captivating and creative.

YouTube gives you an opportunity to get creative and present a commercial about your business to a community of over one hundred million users – for free. Of course, your video production costs are not free, but you may be surprised at how easily you can create your own videos and present them on YouTube. Get creative and you could produce a short "Super Bowl style" commercial about your business that will create a buzz with YouTube viewers.

YouTube is ideal for:

- Introducing your company.
- Promoting your business.
- Providing informative videos for your clients and potential clients.
- Creating a following of potential customers.
- Making new friends.
- Making new business contacts.
- Selling products and services.

To get started on YouTube:

1. Go to YouTube.com.

2. Complete your profile – use your business name or a name that represents your brand.

3. Create your own channel. Use a name that represents your brand and the type of videos to be expected on this channel. If you were selling Science Fiction books, you would pick a name like MySciFiCollection. This way other users can easily find you and follow you to see your latest videos about your business and products when you upload them.

4. Next produce and upload some sample videos.

5. Monitor the traffic or success of each video. Look at how many times each video is viewed and how much traffic you receive to your website as a result.

6. Refine your video offering.

Sometimes the biggest challenge is deciding the topic for your videos. Of course you should browse videos other businesses present on YouTube for great ideas.

Some suggestions to get you started include:

1. Introduce your business and products.

2. Introduce your staff.

3. Show a video of a company gathering with some tasteful but funny events or discussions captured.

4. Create a tour of your office – present your business environment.

5. Provide a how-to video showing use of your products or services.

6. Consider adding something funny or real to any or all of your videos. Get creative suggestions from your co-

workers. Maybe act out something funny that happened in the office and conclude the video promoting a product related to that funny event. Humor can be contagious and result in viral marketing.

7. Promote upcoming events. Show video of a past company event and introduce the next event.

8. Allow your customers to submit questions on your Twitter or Facebook page, and have employees answer the questions on YouTube. Post a link to the video on your Twitter or Facebook page. This will show you're listening to customers.

9. Offer your videos with closed captioning or subtitles in English and Spanish.

10. Create Generation Equis targeted videos in Spanish that add a cultural element.

Some tips on using YouTube include:

1. Create a Spanish channel with videos in Spanish or with Spanish subtitles.

2. Post links to your videos on your other Social Networks.

3. Consider paid promotion of your best videos on YouTube.

4. Run a contest. Get others to submit videos related to your business or products. Perhaps a cash prize for the funniest video using your product.

5. Display your company information in all of your videos. This can be done in a common trailer in each of your videos. Include company name, website address, phone number and e-mail.

6. Comment on other videos.

7. Join other channels related to your business or that represent your potential clients.

Now take what you learned about social networking – and be social! Start participating today in the social networking sites we mentioned. Expand into Generation Equis social sites. Post in Spanish and English.

Also, stay connected to the latest buzz. New social networking sites pop up all the time. Many are targeted towards popular topics. You will likely discover topics that are relevant to your business where you can easily contribute and benefit by joining.

Use the tools we discussed earlier to evaluate the traffic and popularity of the sites you choose to join. This way you make the best use of your time. Wouldn't you rather go to a social gathering where the opportunity to meet the most people is the greatest? The same concept applies to your online activities.

SUMMARY

A QUICK RECAP TO GET YOU STARTED

"Generation Equis – do not waste time, they are waiting. Are you ready?"

Simply put, Generation Equis represents opportunity. After reading this book, you are now prepared to take advantage of this opportunity, with a heightened awareness of this emerging market and key strategies to succeed.

The greatest opportunity exists for those who act right now. Every day you delay your plan to implement the concepts described in this guide represents lost revenues and missed opportunities for you and your company.

Review of the Major Topics

The information presented in this book has been gathered and proven over many years of doing business with Generation Equis.

As you build your plans to tap into this market, review each section carefully. If you still have questions, or would like further information, we invite you to contact us at:

www.GenerationEquisMedia.com.

We want to help others understand what it takes to grow their businesses and achieve competitive advantage by marketing to Generation Equis – the right way.

Now let's review the major topics presented earlier.

Generation Equis

Generation Equis is a label given to the generation of individuals of Hispanic origin who were born after 1960. The majority of this rapidly growing group lives in the United States, but they may also reside in other countries throughout the world. This is perhaps one of the most rapidly growing population groups seen in the last century.

They represent an incredible opportunity for any business or individual who learns how to effectively market and sell to them. Their buying power is expected to exceed one trillion dollars (that is $1,000,000,000.00) in 2010.

The population group is also growing over fifty-percent per year and already represents over 10 percent of the population in the United States alone.

Spanish Website Development

This includes everything from simple landing pages to a complete Spanish website with integration to English websites. The right website development strategy and relevant content are the first things to consider when doing business online with Generation Equis.

Metrics and Reporting

If you have made the investment of time and money in building a new website or modifying your existing website to target Generation Equis, you should also invest in good tracking and metrics. You cannot make marketing decisions, establish metrics and benchmarks or identify areas for improvement unless you have reliable information about visitor behavior.

Search Engine Optimization

Optimizing your website for first page search engine ranking in both the English and Spanish search engines is key to introducing your brand, product or service to Generation Equis via the Internet. Search engines will provide you with the most cost effective and targeted traffic on the web.

Online Messaging

Whenever you are messaging to the visitors to your website, whether you are using email communication or have implemented opt-in methods such as newsletters, it is important to track your visitors' preferences and "speak their language."

For example, if a visitor signs up for a newsletter on your Spanish website it needs to be delivered to them in Spanish and relevant to Generation Equis as defined by the nature of your business and the knowledge of the market that you take away from this book.

Internet Marketing

Depending on your budget, the right combination of Pay Per Click (PPC) and banner advertising, link exchanges, forum and blog posts and traditional media advertising can drive immediate traffic to your website and help you reach out to Generation Equis.

Social Networking

Generation Equis is taking advantage of both the Spanish versions of English sites such as MySpace, Facebook and LinkedIn, as well as the Spanish social media sites such as Sonico and Tuenti. In today's world, an online community presence is just as important to the success of your business as a physical community presence is. Social networking can also be an extremely cost-effective marketing tool, since the cost of entry is so low.

Implementation

If you should decide you need assistance on any of the items discussed in the text of this book, because you do not have the right talent available with your current staff or simply because you want to implement a Generation Equis solution as quickly and cost effectively as possible, please feel free to contact us at: www.GenerationEquisMedia.com.

Be careful that you find a source you can trust should you go elsewhere, and be aware that we practice everything written in this book and are happy to assist you. We wish you success in your online business as you target Generation Equis and the many opportunities this rapidly growing group represents.

Below is handy overview of the types of services required to create a Generation Equis friendly online business:

Business Analysis

The best first step you can take is to have your business evaluated to determine which services could be of benefit to you. It is possible, though not likely, that this could be the last step for you. It is rare to find a business that does not have some room for improvement. The business analysis is targeted towards your goals, so be sure you have a basic idea of what you want to accomplish with your online business before requesting this service.

On completion of the analysis, you should receive a written summary of the conclusions regarding your current or proposed business operation. In addition to the summary, you should also receive a prioritized list of suggested services and their benefits.

You should then meet with the provider of the Business Analysis to review the suggestions and agree to an action plan to move forward with additional services, if they are justified.

Website Analysis

Most active websites on the Internet today are in need of at least some kind of optimization. A website analysis can provide you with valuable information about where you stand. The major areas evaluated during an analysis should at least include:

- Your domain name – Does your domain fit your business and is it search engine friendly?

- Presentation – Does the look and feel properly represent your business?

- Branding – Will people remember you?

- Navigation – Is it easy and intuitive to navigate your website?

- Web crawler friendly – Can search engines find relevant data?

- Search engine optimization – How do you rank?

- Use of advertising – Is your advertising effective?

Depending on the results of this analysis, you may want to take steps to refine your website.

Website Analytics – Metrics & Reporting

If you do not have some sort of reliable analytics program integrated on your website, you are running your business in the dark. When you are ready to manage your business effectively you must integrate some sort of analytics program. This way you can track how your business is doing on the web, and the impact of your ongoing marketing and search engine optimization efforts.

To integrate analytics, code must be added to selected pages of your website that identifies their content for the search engines.

A good analytics program should enable you to track:

- Traffic sources

- Traffic volume

- Return versus new traffic

- Time each visitor spends on your website

- The web pages visited

- The click paths visitors use to navigate your website. This way you can identify the most highly-trafficked paths and optimize them. Click paths can also help you identify areas where your customers may be getting confused, so you can address those issues.

- Summary reports should be available that allow you to drill-down to see additional details as needed.

SEO – Search Engine Optimization

This is the most common service used by online businesses. When optimization is done correctly, it results in free and steady traffic to your website. This service can be focused on Generation Equis, or all Internet users, and typically includes:

- Title tags
- Alt tags
- Keyword-rich text
- Inbound links
- Outbound links
- Search engine submission

Spanish Website Translation

Some businesses want a simple translation of an English website to Spanish. However, most businesses prefer to start from scratch. Either choice is a step in the right direction towards a Generation Equis-friendly website.

When a translation is desired, the translated items could include:

- Website text of all pages
- Meta text, alt tags, etc.

- Messaging used on the website

- Banners with text

- Graphics with text

- If Google AdWords or a similar program are used to generate revenue for the website, change is required to use a Spanish version of advertising

Branding

Branding may involve simply improving your brand or it could be a fresh new start and include any or all of the following:

- A new domain name

- Logo

- Website header with your logo

- Banners with your logo

- Messaging to use your brand

- Marketing ads that use your brand

- Business cards, etc.

Spanish & Traditional Internet Marketing

Marketing your business using traditional and proven strategies to reach Generation Equis can be very effective. Consider the types of marketing listed below. Any or all of these strategies can work for your business and can be custom tailored to fit your budget and growth objectives. The most commonly used online channels include:

- Affiliate programs

- Banner advertising
- Online newspapers and classified ads
- Pay per click – Google & Yahoo
- Forums and groups
- Social networking
- Press releases

Generation Equis Targeted Business Consulting

If you are ready to take the next steps to provide a Generation Equis-friendly web presence, the right online marketing strategies are just as important as any other facet of your business strategy.

Generation Equis Media business consulting service includes everything covered in this book and more. Our services will enable your business to stand apart and help you take advantage of proven strategies for selling and marketing to Generation Equis – online.

If you would like to know more, want to offer feedback or even suggestions for a future publication - please contact us at:

www.GenerationEquisMedia.com

www.ingramcontent.com/pod-product-compliance
Lightning Source LLC
Chambersburg PA
CBHW071142050326
40690CB00008B/1544